Ex Libris

Name —————————————————————

Address —————————————————————

—————————————————————

—————————————————————

Telephone —————————————————————

e-mail —————————————————————

© Kalabindu Enterprises P. Ltd.

ISBN: 978-93-5036-854-1

Kalabindu Enterprises P. Ltd.
GF–18, Virat Bhawan
Commercial Complex, Mukherjee Nagar
Delhi 110009
Phone: +91-11-47038000

A
Nature

NOTEBOOK

Contents

The Miracle of Life

Life, today, in all its diversity is the result of millions of years of evolutionary change. How did this miracle occur? No one knows for sure.

For much of the long span of Earth's history our planet was barren and lifeless. The mysterious journey of life began some 3500 million years ago in the primitive seas in the form of microscopic organisms. They may have been created by the action of sunlight and lightning on chemicals, forming into organic molecules.

The first recognizable organisms were single-celled bacteria and colonies of blue-green algae. From this beginning, through the process of evolution, have come all the wondrous hordes of flying, swimming, crawling and walking creatures, the countless shrubs and trees, mosses and grasses, ferns and flowers and humans.

The first to live on land were plants and primitive insects. Giant dragonflies with huge wingspans of 30 inches hovered over ancient swamps. Insects were also the first to develop wings about 50 million years before birds appeared.

Frogs, toads and salamanders, or the amphibians were the first vertebrates to live on land. But they remained dependent on water and returned to it to lay eggs.

The final steps on land were taken by the reptiles that evolved from amphibians. But some reptiles, crocodiles and sea snakes, lived in water. Among the early reptiles were the spectacular dinosaurs which ruled the earth for more than 200 million years before they disappeared about 65 million years ago. But before that, birds and mammals, the dominant life-forms today, had evolved out of reptilian ancestors.

Although the Earth is 4500 million-years-old, humans appeared only 2 million years ago. They have inherited from animals several systems of behavior which were perfected over millions of years. All creatures learnt to adapt to the environment for the survival of their species.

Animals possess varying degrees of intelligence. Many build homes and care for their young. Many navigate over thousands of miles taking clues from landmarks, the Sun and stars. Animals have also developed amazing systems of defence and communication some of which include ultrasonic sound, inaudible to man.

Without the experiments made in the animal world in adaptation and survival, humans could not have arrived on earth.

The peacock dances displaying its magnificient colors. The shimmering colors are, however, due to refraction and reflection of light by the simple structure of the feathers.

The green turtle 'cries' after coming to land to lay eggs. Tears are a way of removing the extra salt it takes in while feeding and drinking at sea.

The desert-dwelling, water-holding frog absorbs water through its skin and burrows into the sand where it can spend two years until the next rainfall.

The Odyssey of Life

"We are only fellow
voyagers with other creatures
in the odyssey of evolution."

—Aldo Leopold

Events	Period	Year (in Millions)
Origin of earth. Origin of life. Oxygen accumulates in atmosphere. Origin of photosynthesis.	Precambrian	4500
Appearance of invertebrates—jellyfish, worms, molluscs, sponges and trilobites.	Cambrian	600
Appearance of vertebrates. Earliest jawless fishes. First corals.	Ordovician	500
First land plants. First jawed fish.	Silurian	450
First amphibians and insects. First vertebrates on land. Age of fishes. First plants with seeds.	Devonian	400
First reptiles. Great expansion of forests. Amphibians become abundant.	Carboniferous	350
Decline of amphibians. First gymnosperms—plants with cones.	Permian	300
Earliest dinosaurs. Earliest mammals. First tortoises and turtles. Forests of conifers and ferns.	Triassic	250
Earliest bird—archeopteryx. Age of dinosaurs.	Jurassic	200
First flowering plants. Dinosaurs and ammonites become extinct. Early primates. Earliest homonoids, man-like apes.	Cretaceous	150
Forests recede. First deserts. Age of mammals. First horses and elephants. Alps and Himalayas formed. Origin of hominids, ancestors of man (2 million years ago).	Tertiary	50
Appearance of *Homo sapiens* (500,000 years ago). Human civilization.	Quarternary Present time	1.5 –

The eel possesses a well-developed sense of smell, comparable to that of a dog.

The tallest and the largest of all cranes, the Indian Sarus pairs for life. Legend says when one is killed, the other dies of a broken heart.

The several thousand species of ants are specialists in chemical communication. The odor produced after their death immediately motivates the workers to remove the corpses from the nest.

Sounds and Signs

Animals communicate with one another in many interesting ways. These may consist of signs, gestures, looks, sounds, smells or even light produced by the body. Song and dance are the other means of communication.

When faced with danger, animals warn one another using signals such as mock charges, grimaces or sound. They also call their mates, inform other members of the group about the sources of food, advertise territory and 'teach' their young the ways of the world. Baby birds call their parents for help and attention and also to demand food.

Far from being a silent world, the ocean is a noisy place. Fishes, molluscs, sea lions, walruses, whales and dolphins chatter away in the waters using a variety of sounds—whistles, squeaks, clicks and groans which range from low-pitch to ultrasonic sounds beyond the range of human hearing. Whales and dolphins are sometimes called the 'musicians of the sea,' as birds are of the sky.

Many fishes are known to give 'distress calls' when alarmed. Some fishes produce sounds by rubbing together parts of their body as some insects do. Some make a point by grinding their teeth and certain kinds of molluscs do so by striking together their shells.

The use of biological light is one of the most remarkable forms of animal communication as in the case of deep-sea fish of the dark waters and insects such as fireflies and glowworms.

A number of animals also communicate with 'chemical language.' Pheromones are smelly chemicals secreted by some insects to pass messages. Others pick up these messages with the help of antennae carrying the sense organs. Moths, for instance, smell a female miles away and fly to it in the dark. Communication within a termite colony is ensured by using chemical commands.

Mammals communicate largely with facial expressions and sounds. Chimps and gorillas, for example, have a rich repertoire of expressions that reflect different moods.

The position of the ears, tail, type of look and exposure of teeth are also important means of communicating different messages. For instance, when a rabbit senses danger, it thumps the ground with its back legs. A beaver slaps its tail against the water and a gorilla beats its chest.

The wingless female glowworm switches off the light at her hind end at her own sweet will. But when it wants to call its winged mate, it gives out a bright light.

Dance, the language of the bees, communicates directional information about the locations of nectar sources to fellow bees.

Even inside the egg, chicks can react to the different calls of adult birds. And before hatching, a cluster of eggs maintain acoustic contact with one another, so that they all hatch at the same time.

Of Animal Bonds

Almost all birds and mammals, many fishes and some reptiles and amphibians care for their young. Many animals play with their babies and express love by touching and hugging their young.

Most birds and animals clean, feed and protect their babies from lurking enemies. Some prevent the young from heat and cold. Others ensure that their little ones get a regular supply of oxygen. Birds and mammals also 'teach' their fledglings how to go about in the world as adults.

A number of animals build homes for their young. Tailor and weaver birds, ants, wasps and bees are among nature's master designers, engineers and architects. Using twigs, leaves, plant fibers, mud, saliva, wood and wax, they weave, stitch and construct various types of homes for their young. Often a tree is used from top to roots as animal homes.

Some frogs make nests with foams where tadpoles grow up safely. When fully grown, the frogs drop down to the ground and fend for themselves.

Female elephants care the longest for their calves. After a baby is born, it is closely guarded for months and made to walk between the mother and 'aunt' while marching through the jungle tracts.

Male animals of a number of species also share parental duties. The male saltwater crocodile is known to care for babies when mama is out on a swim. At meal times, the chief gorilla keeps watch while the females and the youngsters feed. Later, while the leader eats, older sons keep guard.

Feeding the young is common practice among birds and mammals. Some birds also carry water for their babies. The black vulture fetches water in its mouth and dribbles it down young throats. Some ground nesting birds, the residents of hot regions, stand in the scorching sun with outspread wings providing a cool shade for their nestlings.

To keep babies safe, a number of mammals carry the young from place to place. The giant anteater carries its baby on its back. The baby pangolin rides its mother's tail. Baby tilapias swim into the safety of their mother's mouth when danger threatens.

The animal world is full of outstanding examples of the intimate bond between parents and their young. So deep is this age-old relationship that separation at an early age causes great distress to both.

Bats are masters of acoustic communication. When a young bat calls its mother, the latter can recognize its offspring among tens of thousands of others hanging upside down from the ceilings of caves.

The song thrush keeps its nest clean by removing the droppings of its young; the droppings which are contained in a gelatinous sac. The parents carry and dispose of the sacs at a distance.

Home Sweet Home

A number of animals build homes.

The male **weaver bird,** which dons bright plumage during the breeding season but reverts to its drab color, makes elaborate flask-shaped nests from strands of grass or palm fonds. Each nest is separate, but a single tree may contain hundreds of nests.

Termites build towers 19.5 feet high and 98 feet wide. Ten tons of mud are collected bit by bit by millions of these insects for the mud castle guarded by soldier termites. The queen lays her eggs and is fed by worker termites.

The **wasp** is a skilful builder. Most dig nest-tunnels in the ground or in rotten wood. Some actually build nests with clay. The potter wasp builds a beautiful little clay vase. The nest of the *polistes* wasps is made of lots of little 'rooms' or cells made of paper. The wasps make the paper by chewing wood in their mouths. Bee's cells are made of wax.

Beavers build their lodge with wood and mud in lakes and rivers. They cut down trees by gnawing the trunks into pieces and dragging them into the water to build a dam to make a deep pool. They build their lodge with underwater entrances in the pool, using sticks and mud.

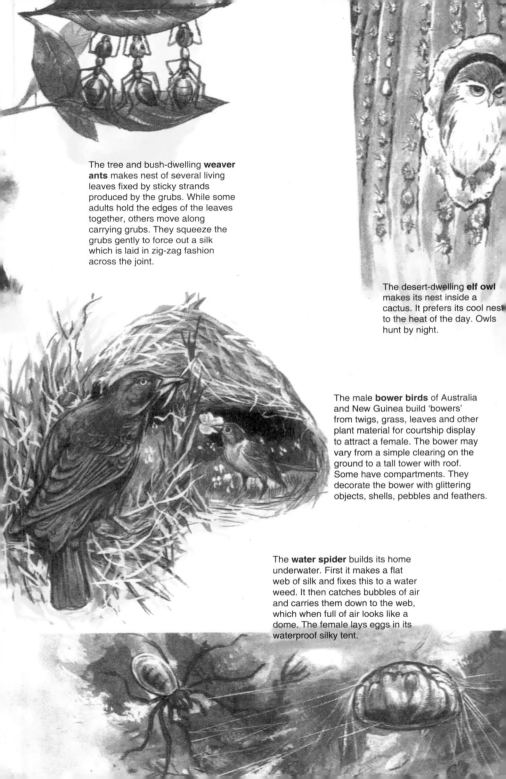

The tree and bush-dwelling **weaver ants** makes nest of several living leaves fixed by sticky strands produced by the grubs. While some adults hold the edges of the leaves together, others move along carrying grubs. They squeeze the grubs gently to force out a silk which is laid in zig-zag fashion across the joint.

The desert-dwelling **elf owl** makes its nest inside a cactus. It prefers its cool nest to the heat of the day. Owls hunt by night.

The male **bower birds** of Australia and New Guinea build 'bowers' from twigs, grass, leaves and other plant material for courtship display to attract a female. The bower may vary from a simple clearing on the ground to a tall tower with roof. Some have compartments. They decorate the bower with glittering objects, shells, pebbles and feathers.

The **water spider** builds its home underwater. First it makes a flat web of silk and fixes this to a water weed. It then catches bubbles of air and carries them down to the web, which when full of air looks like a dome. The female lays eggs in its waterproof silky tent.

The male seahorse is an excellent father. He carries a pouch in his abdomen where the mother lays her eggs. The eggs hatch in about four weeks.

As scorpions are born, their mother carefully twists her pincers to provide them with an easy climb up. The young clamber slowly up the claws and closely packed, ride their mother's back. In case of an accidental fall, the mother stops for the lost one to climb back.

Spikes and Stripes

Most animals need to protect themselves from the attack of predators and, hence, have evolved systems of self and group defense. In the war against enemies, animal weaponry ranges from armor such as spikes, claws, shells, horns, bony plates to poisonous chemicals that kill; they can cause burns or irritations too. Tricks and mimicry are also used to confuse the enemy and send it away.

Color and patterns on an animal's coat are also important means of self-defense in the animal kingdom and are used to warn rivals and frighten an enemy or to hide. The use of color and body pattern—dots, stripes and spots help the animal merge with the background and, thus, escape notice when the hunter is around. This is called camouflage.

Camouflage is also used by the hunter to disguise its presence while stalking a prey. Lines and dots help tigers and leopards to conceal themselves while hunting.

Some animals also change color to blend with the background. The chameleon, for instance, turns red, yellow, black or multicolored. Some octopuses can make their skin bumpy to match a similar background.

Several animals have developed lethal defence systems using poisonous stings, sprays and bites to injure or kill an enemy. Snakes (some species only), scorpions, wasps, jellyfish and stingrays are poisonous. So is the heavily camouflaged stonefish.

Most animals defend themselves by escaping from the enemy. The strategies used are to freeze, sham death, flee or finally fight. As the eyes of the predator can detect the slightest movement, the hare remains motionless in self-defense. This 'statue' game is also played by the tree squirrel.

A number of animals fool their enemies by pretending to be an unpalatable dish. Some spiders mimic ants by lifting up their front legs like the feelers of an ant, which few fancy eating because of their bad taste.

And some creatures—the stick and leaf insects and the flower mantis save themselves from predators because their bodies are shaped like twig, leaf or a flower. A number of animals also make themselves look bigger and fiercer. The Australian frill-lizard, frightens its enemy by suddenly spreading out its neck frill and opening its mouth wide.

Pigeons provide a unique drink called 'crop-milk.' The lining of their crop, that is, the baglike part of the bird's throat becomes so swollen with a white liquid that the cells burst. The young birds suck this unusual form of sustenance.

Nesting fish ensure that their little ones get enough oxygen by spending many hours fanning a current of water over their nests by beating with their fins. Others gurgle the young in their mouths as a way of increasing the oxygen supply.

Going Places

Since millions of years many species of mammals, birds, fishes and insects have been seasonally migrating along air, land and water routes from colder to warmer areas in search of food and hospitable weather. The long journeys some of them undertake across continents, mountains, deserts, rivers and seas are simply spectacular.

Come winter and myriads of birds fly across the skies, while wetlands, rivers, ponds and gardens become dotted with twittering feathered beings. Where do the wagtails, storks and waterfowls come from?

As temperatures dip, nearly a third of all birds of the Northern Hemisphere migrate from their temperate homes to warmer regions of the south, covering thousands of miles. When spring arrives, they return to their nesting grounds. For the long distances they cover, birds build up enormous fat reserves before departure, some actually doubling their weight and converting fat into energy during flight.

More than 500 species of migratory birds are known to come to India every winter along the western Indus and the Brahmaputra Valley approach. The bar-headed geese fly across the Himalayas at a height of 26,000 feet. However, most birds fly below

260 feet at a speed of 18–62 miles per hour. A number of birds also migrate within the country.

Besides birds gnus, elephants, caribous, bats, wolves, whales, dolphins and eels also undertake migration. The fragile butterfly can travel more than 37,000 miles in a lifetime. The Monarch butterfly flies from Canada to Mexico every year.

Among migratory fishes, eels are the most fascinating. Spending their lives in rivers, they swim for miles into the sea to lay eggs. The young after hatching return to the rivers, while the parents die in the sea.

How do animals navigate across the skies, oceans and continents? Some orient themselves according to the Sun's position, using it as a compass. Animals that travel by night are directed by starlight and moonlight. Birds are also guided by the magnetic field of the Earth in combination with gravity. While salmons, that move upstream to spawn use their sense of smell to find their way to the spot where they had hatched.

Scientists continue to study the fascinating phenomenon of animal migration.

Flight is a common means of self-defense. Antelopes flee at 45 miles an hour, while the deer have been recorded to sustain a speed of 30 miles per hour for an astonishing 20 miles.

Birds of prey may nosedive at speeds of up to 110 miles an hour. The best defense system against aerial attack that some animals have evolved is the quick scamper down tunnels into their burrows.

Winging Across

The map below shows the migratory paths of four birds visiting India every winter.

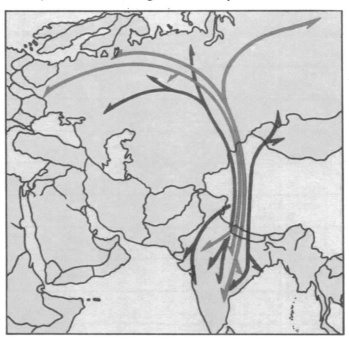

Courtesy: Survey of India, Dept. of Science and Technology

▬ **White Stork**　▬ **Rosy Pastor**　▬ **Brown-headed Gull**　▬ **Spotted Sandpiper**

The **white stork** from west Asia and central Europe comes to India in September covering 3700 miles. It returns home in April.

The **brown-headed gull** from central Asia and Tibet flies to India in September and returns home in April.

The **rosy pastor** breeds in eastern Europe and central western Asia. It comes to India in August and returns by April.

The **spotted sandpiper** breeds in Europe and northern Asia, migrating to India in September, and returning in April.

Mysterious Flyways

This map shows the migratory paths of the golden plover and the Arctic tern.

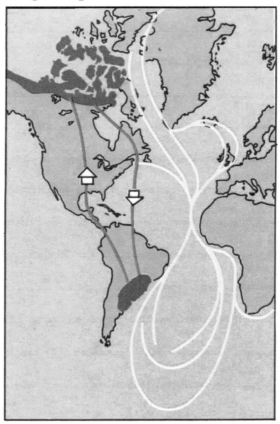

Golden Plover ▬▬▬ Arctic Tern

The **golden plover** is a famous bird traveler. It spends its summer in northern Canada and Alaska, then flies nonstop over the Atlantic to Argentina for the winter. It returns via a different route making a loop.

The **Arctic tern**, one of the greatest bird wanderers, nests within 8° of the North Pole. In fall it migrates to the Antarctic, returning again in spring. The round journey may be over 22,000 miles.

When threatened, a grass snake hisses and strikes with its mouth shut. If that fails to scare an enemy, it produces a foul smell. Finally, it will sham death.

The most virulent poison from the animal world comes from the skin of small, brightly colored poison-arrow frogs of South American forests. One gram of this toxin is enough to kill a hundred thousand average-sized men.

Extinctions

Since the dim past the journey of life has been punctuated by extinctions of species. Collision of meteorites, volcanic eruptions, continental drifts and environmental changes have all resulted in the disappearance of life forms from Earth from time to time. Trilobites, ammonites and dinosaurs were all victims of mass extinction.

In nature, extinction has been part of the evolutionary process. It has heralded the arrival of advanced life forms. For instance, although mammals appeared during the time of the dinosaurs, they remained tiny and subdued until the dinosaurs vanished. Then mammals came centerstage, showing up in a great variety of forms.

Since the arrival of man, the greatest predator on Earth, the rate of extinction has drastically increased. The great mammals of the past such as the mastodon, mammoth, saber-toothed cat, giant lemur, giant and ground sloth, all disappeared as humans advanced.

Nothing in the past matches the present day record of destruction of species at the hands of man. An estimated million species will be lost in the next twenty-five years. Man's destructive activities—logging, fire, deforestation, overuse of natural resources and wanton killing for economic gain are resulting in biological damage of a most serious form.

Since the beginning of the industrial era, several species of animals have become extinct. A number of microorganisms have disappeared even before they could be identified.

The Mauritian dodo, the North American passenger pigeon, the elephant bird of Madagascar, the painted vulture of Florida, the cape lion and the quagga of South Africa are all gone. In India, the cheetah, the lesser one-horned rhinoceros, the pink-headed duck and the mountain quail have vanished during this century. At the present estimate, 86 species of mammals, 70 of birds and 28 of amphibians and reptiles are considered endangered in India.

Naturalists say, "There is nothing in Nature to prove that it cares more for our human species than for daffodils... If endangered by us, Nature will strike back."

Presumably the great journey of life will go on. Fortunately, today, we have begun to marvel at the miracle that is life and made conservation our motto.

A frightenend squid squirts a kind of ink into the water that spreads like a black cloud and hides the squid. The squid then escapes. Some deep-sea squids make a luminous cloud to dazzle the enemy.

The leaf-cutter ant carries out long-distance movements to obtain suitable pieces of plant material to cultivate the fungi on which it lives.

The Earth's champion flier, the Arctic tern, flies every winter from its home in the North Pole to coastal areas of the Antarctic. In spring the great journey home is repeated, covering a total distance of 22,000 miles while flying pole to pole twice every year.

Thoughts on Nature

"Twenty-six years after my coronation I have declared that many animals must be protected. These are birds like parrots, mynahs, ruddy geese, wild pigeons, domestic pigeons and wild ducks and creatures like bats, queen ants, terrapins, boneless fish, tortoises, porcupines, squirrels, deer, bulls and wild asses. All four-footed creatures that are neither useful nor edible should also be protected."

ASHOKA

"I believe all animals were provided by God to help keep man alive."

IWAO FUJITA

"Cats and monkeys, monkeys and cats, all human life is there."

HENRY JAMES

"There is a sufficiency in the world for man's need but not for man's greed."

MOHANDAS K. GANDHI

"We cannot command Nature except by obeying her."

FRANCIS BACON

"Man maketh a death which Nature never made."

EDWARD YOUNG

"Nature provides a free lunch, but only if we control our appetites."

WILLIAM RUCKELSHAUS

"The earth we abuse and the living things we kill will, in the end, take their revenge; for in exploiting their presence we are diminishing our future."

MARYA MANNES

"We say we love flowers, yet we pluck them. We say we love trees, yet we cut them down. And people still wonder why some are afraid when told they are loved."

ANONYMOUS

India—Wildlife

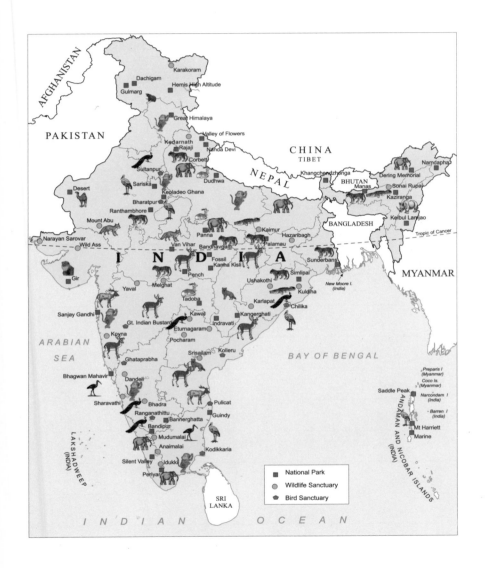

When spiny lobsters migrate, they adopt a curious single-file procession. Following one after the other, they make their way to the breeding grounds, where each female lays about 15,000 eggs.

When gnus begin their annual migration, they gather in enormous herds, which also includes other species of animals such as the antelope, zebra and even the ostrich.

With their enormous daily requirements for food and water, elephants keep constantly on the move, sometimes taking several years to return to their point of origin.

Biodiversity

India's Biological Diversity*
(known species)

Group	No. of species
Mammals	390
Reptiles	456
Fishes	2546
Molluscs	5070
Birds	1232
Amphibians	209
Flowering Plants	15,000

*Source: Internet

Bibliography

ALI, SALIM *The Book of Indian Birds,* Bombay, BNHS, Oxford University Press, 1941

BEDI, RAJESH & RAMESH *Indian Wildlife,* New Delhi, 1984

CHINERY, MICHAEL ed. *Dictionary of Animals,* London, Kingfisher Books, 1984

DAY, DAVID *The Encyclopaedia of Vanished Species,* Hong Kong, Mclaren Publishing, 1981

GAMLIN, LINDA *Evolution,* London, Dorling Kindersley, 1993

GEE, E. P. *The Wildlife of India,* London, Collins, 1964

HARLOW, EVE & PARSONS, IAIN *The Encyclopaedia of Wildlife,* London, Salamander Books, 1974

JINDAL, S. L. *Flowering Shrubs in India,* New Delhi, Publications Division, 1970

MORRIS, DESMOND *Animal Watching, A Field Guide to Animal Behavior,* London, Jonathan Cape, 1990

NAIR, S. M. *Endangered Animals of India and their Conservation,* New Delhi, NBT, 1992

PRATER, S. H. *The Book of Indian Animals,* Bombay, BNHS, 1971

SESHADRI, B. *India's Wildlife and Wildlife Reserves.* New Delhi, Sterling Publishers, 1986

SCHAUENBERG, PAUL *Animal Communication,* London, Burke Books, 1981

SCHALLER, G. B. *The Deer and the Tiger: A Study of Wildlife in India,* Chicago, 1967

SINGH, ARJUN *Tiger Haven,* London, Macmillan, 1973

TIKADER, B. K. *Threatened Animals of India,* Calcutta, Zoological Survey of India, 1983

WITAKER, ZAI & ROMULUS *The Snakes Around Us,* New Delhi, NBT, 1986

Photo: Vivek